10/07

ALL ABOUT FALL

Animals in Fall

by Martha E. H. Rustad

Consulting Editor: Gail Saunders-Smith, PhD

CAPSTONE *press*®

Mankato, Minnesota

Pebble Plus is published by Capstone Press,
151 Good Counsel Drive, P.O. Box 669, Mankato, Minnesota 56002.
www.capstonepress.com

1 2 3 4 5 6 12 11 10 09 08 07

Library of Congress Cataloging-in-Publication Data
Rustad, Martha E. H. (Martha Elizabeth Hillman), 1975–
    Animals in fall / by Martha E. H. Rustad.
    p. cm. — (Pebble plus. All about fall)
    Summary: "Simple text and photographs present animals in fall"—Provided by publisher.
    Includes bibliographical references and index.
    ISBN-13: 978-1-4296-0022-4 (hardcover)
    ISBN-10: 1-4296-0022-5 (hardcover)
    1. Animal behavior—Juvenile literature. 2. Autumn—Juvenile literature. I. Title. II. Series.
QL751.5.R87 2008
578.4'3—dc22   2006102052

Editorial Credits

Sarah L. Schuette, editor; Veronica Bianchini, designer; Charlene Deyle, photo researcher

Photo Credits

Bruce Coleman Inc./Warren Photographic, 13
Corbis/Buddy Mays, 21; Charles Mauzy, 19; Kennan Ward, 11; Kevin Schafer, 15; Tim Davis, 7
Shutterstock/Dainis Derics, 17; Eric Gevaert, 5; Gilles DeCruyenaere, cover; Mark C. Biesinger, 1
SuperStock, Inc./age fotostock, 9

Note to Parents and Teachers

The All about Fall set supports national science standards related to changes during the
seasons. This book describes and illustrates animals in fall. The images support early
readers in understanding the text. The repetition of words and phrases helps early
readers learn new words. This book also introduces early readers to subject-specific
vocabulary words, which are defined in the Glossary section. Early readers may need
assistance to read some words and to use the Table of Contents, Glossary, Read More,
Internet Sites, and Index sections of the book.

Table of Contents

Fall Is Here

It's fall.

Animals start to get ready
for cooler weather.

What Animals Do

Geese know winter is coming.

They fly south together.

6

Monarch butterflies
fly south too.
They find warm places
to stay.

Snowshoe hares change color. Their fur starts to turn from brown to white.

Deer grow thicker coats.
Thick fur keeps them warm
in the cold.

Getting Ready

Squirrels get ready
for winter too.
They hide nuts to eat later.

Honey bees

make extra honey.

They store it in their hives.

Bears eat extra food.

They look for dens to rest.

A New Season

The animals are ready
for winter.
The new season
will begin soon.

Glossary

coat—an animal's fur

den—the home of a wild animal; bears rest in dens in caves or hollow tree trunks.

hare—a mammal like a large rabbit with long, strong back legs

hive—a place where a group of bees live together; bees build honeycombs in hives.

honey—a sweet, sticky, yellow substance made by bees

season—one of the four parts of the year; the seasons are spring, summer, fall, and winter.

weather—the conditions outside at a certain time and place

Read More

Latta, Sara L. *What Happens in Fall?* I Like the Seasons! Berkeley Heights, N.J.: Enslow Elementary, 2006.

Schuette, Sarah L. *Let's Look at Fall.* Pebble Plus: Investigate the Seasons. Mankato, Minn.: Capstone Press, 2007.

Internet Sites

FactHound offers a safe, fun way to find Internet sites related to this book. All of the sites on FactHound have been researched by our staff.

Here's how:

1. Visit *www.facthound.com*

2. Choose your grade level.

3. Type in this book ID **1429600225** for age-appropriate sites. You may also browse subjects by clicking on letters, or by clicking on pictures and words.

4. Click on the **Fetch It** button.

FactHound will fetch the best sites for you!

Index

Word Count: 100
Grade: 1
Early-Intervention Level: 12

24